U.S. Department of Justice
Office of Justice Programs
Bureau of Justice Statistics

MARCH 2013

I0489260

SPECIAL REPORT

NCJ 241291

Hate Crime
Victimization, 2003-2011

Nathan Sandholtz, *BJS Intern*, Lynn Langton, Ph.D., and Michael Planty, Ph.D., *BJS Statisticians*

List of Figures

List of Tables

List of Appendix Tables

U.S. Department of Justice
Office of Justice Programs
Bureau of Justice Statistics

MARCH 2013

NCJ 241291

Hate Crime
Victimization, 2003-2011

Nathan Sandholtz, *BJS Intern*, Lynn Langton, Ph.D., and Michael Planty, Ph.D., *BJS Statisticians*

From 2007 to 2011, an estimated annual average of 259,700 nonfatal violent and property hate crime victimizations occurred against persons age 12 or older residing in U.S. households. Of these hate crimes, victims perceived that the offender was motivated by bias against the victim's religion in 21% of victimizations. The percentage of hate crimes motivated by religious bias more than doubled in 2007-11, compared to the 10% motivated by religious bias in 2003-06 (figure 1). In comparison, the percentage of hate crimes motivated by racial bias was slightly lower in 2007-11 (54%) than in 2003-06 (63%).

The findings from this report came primarily from the Bureau of Justice Statistics' (BJS) National Crime Victimization Survey (NCVS), which has been collecting data on crimes motivated by hate since 2003. The NCVS and the FBI's Uniform Crime Reports (UCR) Hate Crime Statistics Program, which are the principal sources of annual information on hate crime in the United States, use the definition of hate crime provided in the Hate Crime Statistics Act (28 U.S.C. § 534). The act defines hate crimes as "crimes that manifest evidence of prejudice based on race, gender or gender identity, religion, disability, sexual orientation, or ethnicity." The NCVS measures crimes perceived by victims to be motivated by an offender's bias against them for belonging to or being associated with a group largely identified by these characteristics.

FIGURE 1
Victim perceptions of offender bias in hate crime, 2003–2006 and 2007–2011

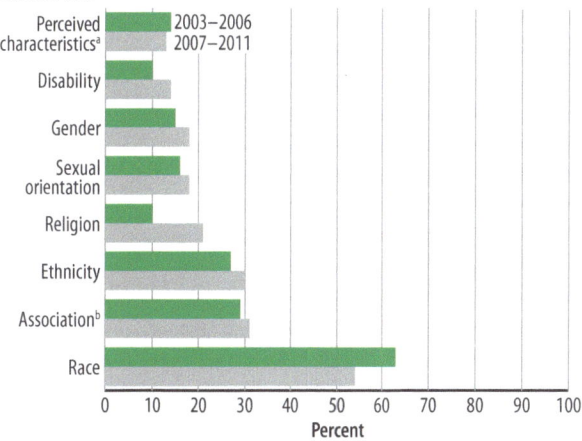

Note: Hate crime includes incidents confirmed by police as bias-motivated and incidents perceived by victims to be bias-motivated because the offender used hate language or left behind hate symbols. Detail does not sum to 100% due to victims reporting more than one type of bias motivating the hate-related victimizations. See appendix table 2 for standard errors.
[a]Motivated by offender's perception of victim's characteristics.
[b]Motivated by victim's association with people having certain characteristics.
Source: Bureau of Justice Statistics, National Crime Victimization Survey, 2003–2011.

HIGHLIGHTS

- Across the periods from 2003-06 and 2007-11, there was no change in the annual average number of total, violent, or property hate crime victimizations.

- The percentage of hate crimes motivated by religious bias more than doubled between 2003-06 and 2007-11 (from 10% to 21%), while the percentage motivated by racial bias dropped slightly (from 63% to 54%).

- Violent hate crime accounted for a higher percentage of all nonfatal violent crime in 2007-11 (4%), compared to 2003-06 (3%).

- About 92% of all hate crimes collected by the NCVS between 2007 and 2011 were violent victimizations.

- About a third of hate crime victimizations occurred at or near the victim's home.

- Between 2003-06 and 2007-11, the percentage of hate crime victimizations reported to police declined from 46% to 35%.

- In 2007-11, whites, blacks, and Hispanics had similar rates of violent hate crime victimization.

Changes to the measurement of hate crime in the NCVS

Since the release of the previous BJS report on hate crime victimization (*Hate Crime, 2003-2009*, NCJ 234085, June 2011), BJS has instituted two changes to the measurement of hate crime using NCVS data. Beginning with the 2010 NCVS data, BJS modified the approach for counting high frequency repeat victimizations, or series victimizations. Series victimizations are those that are similar in type but occur with such frequency that a victim is unable to recall each individual event or to describe each event in detail. Survey procedures allow NCVS interviewers to identify and classify these similar victimizations as series victimizations and collect detailed information on only the most recent incident in the series. Prior to the release of the 2010 NCVS data, BJS counted series victimizations as one victimization. In order to capture these events, BJS now counts series victimizations as the number of incidents experienced by the victim, up to a maximum of 10 (see *Methodology*).

This new approach to counting series victimizations impacts trends in the rate of violent hate crime victimization. With the previous approach to counting series victimizations, the rate of violent hate crime victimizations declined slightly from 2008 to 2010 and stabilized from 2010 to 2011 **(figure 2)**. In comparison, when series victimizations are counted up to a maximum of 10 victimizations, the rate of violent hate crime victimizations was stable from 2008 to 2010 and declined slightly from 2010 to 2011. Regardless of the approach used for counting hate crime victimizations, no significant change was observed in the rate of violent hate crime victimization in 2011 compared to 2004.

The second change to the measurement of hate crime is the inclusion of gender or gender identity bias in the hate crime definition. In 2009, the passage of the Matthew Shepard and James Byrd, Jr. Hate Crimes Prevention Act made gender, gender identity, and sexual orientation protected categories under federal hate crime statutes. The Hate Crime Statistics Act was also amended to reflect the newly protected categories of sexual orientation, gender, and gender identity.

BJS and the FBI have been collecting and reporting on hate crimes motivated by bias against a victim's sexual orientation since 2003. BJS has also previously reported on hate crimes motivated by gender bias when the victim reported an additional bias motivation (e.g., racial or ethnic bias, as well as gender bias). However, beginning with 2010, BJS began including crimes motivated solely by gender or gender identity bias in the hate crime statistics.

The inclusion of crimes motivated solely by gender or gender identity bias did not significantly change the number or rate of hate crime victimizations in 2010 or 2011 **(table 1)**.

FIGURE 2
Rate of violent hate crime victimizations, by method used to count high frequency repeat (series) victimizations, 2004–2011

Rate per 1,000 persons age 12 or older

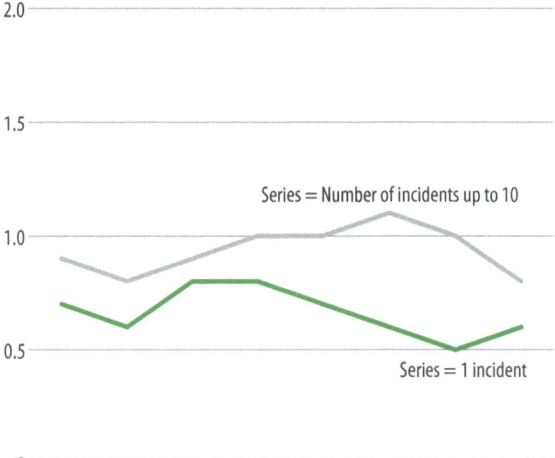

Note: Estimates are based on 2-year rolling averages centered on the most recent year. Hate crime includes incidents confirmed by police as bias-motivated and incidents perceived by victims to be bias-motivated because the offender used hate language or left behind hate symbols. See appendix table 1 for base population numbers and appendix table 3 for estimates and standard errors.

Source: Bureau of Justice Statistics, National Crime Victimization Survey, 2003–2011.

TABLE 1
Violent hate crimes, excluding and including gender bias, 2010–2011

Year	Number		Rate per 1,000 persons age 12 or older	
	Excluding gender bias	Including gender bias	Excluding gender bias	Including gender bias
Annual average	187,450	195,500	0.7	0.8
2010	193,710	196,620	0.8	0.8
2011	181,190	194,390	0.7	0.8

Note: Hate crime includes incidents confirmed by police as bias-motivated and incidents perceived by victims to be bias-motivated because the offender used hate language or left behind hate symbols. Violent hate crimes include rape and sexual assault, robbery, aggravated assault, and simple assault. Numbers rounded to the nearest ten. See appendix table 1 for base population numbers and appendix table 4 for standard errors.

Source: Bureau of Justice Statistics, National Crime Victimization Survey, 2010–2011.

Hate crime victimization refers to a single victim or household that experienced a criminal incident believed to be motivated by hate. For violent crimes (rape or sexual assault, robbery, aggravated assault, and simple assault) and for personal larceny, the count of hate crime victimizations is the number of individuals who experienced a violent hate crime. For crimes against households (burglary, motor vehicle theft, or other theft), each household affected by a hate crime is counted as a single victimization.

This report presents NCVS data on the characteristics of hate crimes and hate crime victims from 2003 to 2011. Trend estimates are based on 2-year rolling averages centered on the most recent year. For example, estimates reported for 2011 represent the average estimates for 2010 and 2011. Subgroup estimates are aggregated annual estimates for two periods—2003 to 2006 and 2007 to 2011. This approach increases the reliability and stability of estimates, which facilitates comparing estimates over time. The report also presents comparisons between the NCVS and the UCR in terms of overall trends in hate crime victimization and the type of bias that motivated the crime.

As a percentage of total violent crime, violent hate crime was greater in 2007-11 (4%) than in 2003-06 (3%)

Overall, the total number of hate crime victimizations remained stable from 2004 to 2011 (table 2). Across the periods from 2003-06 and 2007-11, no change was detected in the annual average number of total, violent, or property hate crime victimizations (table 3). However, violent hate crimes accounted for a higher percentage of all nonfatal violent victimizations in the 2007-11 period (4%) than in the 2003-06 period (3%).

For both periods, the rate of violent hate crime victimization remained unchanged at about 0.9 victimizations per 1,000 persons age 12 or older. The rate of property hate crime victimization was between 0.2 and 0.3 victimizations per 1,000 households in both periods. (Data do not include arson or vandalism.)

TABLE 3
Annual average distribution for hate crime victimizations, by offense, 2003–2006 and 2007–2011

Annual hate crimes	2003–2006	2007–2011
Number[a]	256,080	259,690
Violent[b]	215,900	237,920
Property[c]	38,720	20,990
Percent of all crimes		
Total crime[a]	0.9%	1.1%
Violent crime[b]	2.9	4.0
Property crime[c]	0.2	0.1
Rate		
Violent[b,d]	0.9	0.9
Property[b,e]	0.3	0.2

Note: Hate crime includes incidents confirmed by police as bias-motivated and incidents perceived by victims to be bias-motivated because the offender used hate language or left behind hate symbols. Numbers rounded to the nearest ten. See appendix table 6 for standard errors.

[a]Includes violent crimes, personal larceny, and household property crimes. In 2003-06 there were 108.4 million total victimizations. In 2007-11 there were 114.9 million total victimizations.

[b]Includes rape and sexual assault, robbery, aggravated assault, and simple assault. In 2003-06 there were 836,000 violent victimizations. In 2007-11 there were 834,000 violent victimizations.

[c]Includes burglary, motor vehicle theft, and other theft. In 2003-06 there were 77.8 million property crime victimizations. In 2007-11 there were 84.5 million property crime victimizations.

[d]Per 1,000 persons age 12 or older.

[e]Per 1,000 households.

Source: Bureau of Justice Statistics, National Crime Victimization Survey, 2003–2011.

TABLE 2
Hate crime victimizations, 2004–2011

Year	Total hate crimes[a]		Violent hate crimes[b]			Property hate crimes[c]		
	Number	Percent of total victimizations[d]	Number	Rate[e]	Percent of total violent victimizations[d]	Number	Rate[f]	Percent of total property victimizations[d]
2004	281,670	1.0%	220,060	0.9	3.1%	61,610	0.5	0.3%
2005	223,060	0.9	198,400	0.8	2.9	21,740	0.2	0.1
2006	230,490	0.8	211,730	0.9	2.8	15,830	0.1	0.1
2007	263,440	1.0	236,860	1.0	3.1	24,640	0.2	0.1
2008	266,640	1.1	241,800	1.0	3.7	22,890	0.2	0.1
2009	284,620	1.2	267,170	1.1	4.4	17,450	0.1	0.1
2010	273,100	1.3	255,810	1.0	4.8	17,290	0.1	0.1
2011	217,640	1.0	195,500	0.8	3.6	22,140	0.2	0.1

Note: Hate crime includes incidents confirmed by police as bias-motivated and incidents perceived by victims to be bias-motivated because the offender used hate language or left behind hate symbols. Estimates based on 2-year rolling averages centered on the most recent year. Numbers rounded to the nearest ten. See appendix table 1 for population data and appendix table 5 for standard errors.

[a]Includes violent crimes, personal larceny, and household property crimes.

[b]Includes rape and sexual assault, robbery, aggravated assault, and simple assault.

[c]Includes household burglary, motor vehicle theft, and other theft.

[d]See appendix table 1 for number of total victimizations.

[e]Per 1,000 persons age 12 or older.

[f]Per 1,000 households.

Source: Bureau of Justice Statistics, National Crime Victimization Survey, 2003–2011.

Violent victimizations accounted for 92% of all hate crimes in 2007-11

The percentage of hate crimes that involved violence was greater in 2007-11 (92%) than in 2003-06 (84%) (table 4). Property crimes accounted for a lower percentage of hate crime victimizations in 2007-11 (8%), compared to 2003-06 (15%). The lower percentage of property hate crime victimizations in 2003-06 was driven by a decline in hate-related burglaries. Hate-related burglaries accounted for 2% of all hate crimes during 2007-11 and 9% of all hate crimes during 2003-06.

While a greater percentage of hate crimes were violent victimizations in 2007-11 than in 2003-06, the opposite was true for nonhate crimes. The percentage of nonhate crimes that were violent victimizations declined from 2003-06 to 2007-11 (not shown in a table). Overall, from 2003 through 2011, violent crimes accounted for a greater percentage of hate crimes than nonhate crimes (figure 3).

The percentage of violent hate crimes resulting in victim injury declined over time

In 2007-11, the offender had a weapon in at least 25% of violent hate crime victimizations, and the victim sustained an injury in about 17% of violent hate crime victimizations (table 5). No differences were detected in the percentage of hate crime victimizations in which the offender was known to have a weapon between the 2003-06 and 2007-11 periods. However, the victim sustained an injury in a slightly higher percentage of violent hate crime victimizations in 2003-06 (25%) than in 2007-11 (17%).

TABLE 4
Hate crime victimizations, by type of crime, 2003–2006 and 2007–2011

Type of crime[a]	2003–2006	2007–2011
Violent	84%	92%
Serious violent	23	29
Rape/sexual assault	1 !	3 !
Robbery	5 !	8
Aggravated assault	17	19
Simple assault	61	62
Property[b]	15%	8%
Burglary	9	2 !
Theft	7	6

Note: Hate crime includes incidents confirmed by police as bias motivated and incidents perceived by victims to be bias motivated because the offender used hate language or left behind hate symbols. See appendix table 7 for standard errors.
! Interpret with caution; estimate based on 10 or fewer cases, or the coefficient of variation is greater than 50%.
[a]Personal larceny is not shown. It accounted for about 1% of hate crime victimizations in 2003–06 and less than 0.5% in 2007–11.
[b]Motor vehicle theft is included in property crime total but not shown in the table due to the small percentage of hate crimes involving motor vehicle theft.
Source: Bureau of Justice Statistics, National Crime Victimization Survey, 2003–2011.

TABLE 5
Presence of weapons and injuries sustained in violent hate crime victimizations, 2003–2006 and 2007–2011

Weapon/injury	2003–2006	2007–2011
Weapon	100%	100%
Yes	21	25
No	68	67
Don't know	11	8
Injury	100%	100%
None	75	83
Any*	25	17

Note: Includes incidents confirmed by police as hate crimes or perceived by victims as motivated by bias because the offender used hate language or left behind hate symbols. See appendix table 9 for standard errors.
*Includes minor injuries, rape injuries, and serious injuries (broken bones, lost teeth, internal injuries, loss of consciousness, and any unspecified injury requiring 2 or more days of hospitalization).
Source: Bureau of Justice Statistics, National Crime Victimization Survey, 2003–2011.

FIGURE 3
Hate and nonhate victimizations, by type of crime, 2003–2011

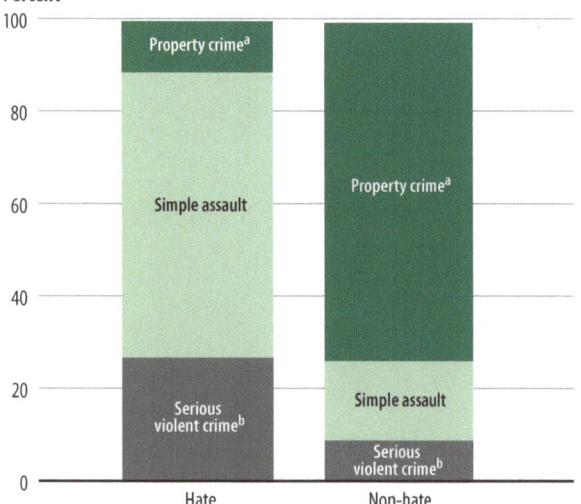

Note: Hate crime includes incidents confirmed by police as bias-motivated and incidents perceived by victims to be bias-motivated because the offender used hate language or left behind hate symbols. See appendix table 8 for estimates and standard errors.
[a]Includes burglary, motor vehicle theft, and other theft.
[b]Includes rape and sexual assault, robbery, and aggravated assault.
Source: Bureau of Justice Statistics, National Crime Victimization Survey, 2003–2011.

About 30% of hate crime victimizations occurred at or near the victim's home

The locations in which hate crimes occurred did not change significantly from 2003-06 to 2007-11 (table 6). During both periods, about a third of hate crime victimizations occurred at or near the victim's home. In 2007-11, about 24% of hate crime victimizations occurred in public places (such as parking lots, on the street, or on public transportation) and about 19% occurred at school.

From 2003 to 2011, the overall percentage of violent nonhate victimizations (36%) that occurred at or near the victim's home was greater than the percentage of violent hate victimizations (27%) that occurred at or near the victim's home (figure 4). In comparison, the percentage of violent hate crimes that occurred in commercial places (16%) and at school (22%) was greater than the percentage of nonhate crimes occurring in these locations. A similar percentage of hate (24%) and nonhate (22%) violent crimes occurred in parking lots, on the street, or on public transportation.

The percentage of hate crimes reported to police declined over time

The percentage of all hate crime victimizations reported to police declined from 46% in 2003-06 to 35% in 2007-11 (table 7). The percentage of violent hate crimes reported to police was 36% in 2007-11.

The decline in the percentage of total hate crimes reported to police was partially attributed to a drop in reporting by persons other than the victim, such as other household members or bystanders. In 2003-06, someone other than the victim reported 21% percent of hate crime victimizations, compared to 11% in 2007-11. About a quarter of all hate crime victimizations were reported to police by the victim, which was consistent across both time periods.

The percentage of violent hate crime victimizations that resulted in the victim signing a complaint remained stable at about 10% from 2003-06 to 2007-11. However, the percentage of violent hate crimes that resulted in an arrest declined from 10% in 2003-06 to 4% in 2007-11.

FIGURE 4
Violent hate and nonhate victimizations, by location, 2003–2011

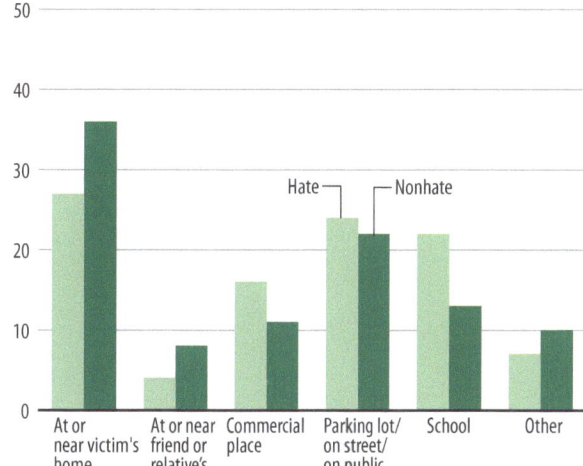

Note: Hate crime includes incidents confirmed by police as bias-motivated and incidents perceived by victims to be bias-motivated because the offender used hate language or left behind hate symbols. See appendix table 11 for estimates and standard errors.
Source: Bureau of Justice Statistics, National Crime Victimization Survey, 2003–2011.

TABLE 6
Hate crime victimizations, by location, 2003–2006 and 2007–2011

Location	2003–2006	2007–2011
At or near victim's home	30%	33%
At or near friend or relative's home	5	3 !
Commercial place	12	16
Parking lot/on street/on public transportation	20	24
School	24	19
Other	9	5

Note: Hate crime includes incidents confirmed by police as bias-motivated and incidents perceived by victims to be bias-motivated because the offender used hate language or left behind hate symbols. Hate crimes include violent crimes, personal larceny, and household property crimes. See appendix table 10 for standard errors.
! Interpret with caution; estimate based on 10 or fewer cases, or the coefficient of variation is greater than 50%.
Source: Bureau of Justice Statistics, National Crime Victimization Survey, 2003–2011.

TABLE 7
Hate crime victimizations reported to police, 2003–2006 and 2007–2011

	Total		Violent	
	2003–2006	2007–2011	2003–2006	2007–2011
Reported by[a]—	46%	35%	43%	36%
Victim	25	24	19	24
Someone else[b]	21	11	24	11
Complaint signed[c]	12%	10%	13%	10%
Arrest made[c]	9%	4%	10%	4%
Not reported[a]	53%	65%	56%	64%

Note: Hate crime includes incidents confirmed by police as bias-motivated and incidents perceived by victims to be bias-motivated because the offender used hate language or left behind hate symbols. Hate crimes include violent crimes, personal larceny, and household property crimes. See appendix table 12 for standard errors.
[a]The percentage of victims (1% or less) who did not know whether the police were notified is not shown in the table.
[b]Includes other household members; other officials, such as guards, apartment managers, and school officials; and others.
[c]Percentages based on all hate crime victimizations, including those in which the police were not notified or it was unknown whether the police were notified.
Source: Bureau of Justice Statistics, National Crime Victimization Survey, 2003–2011.

From 2003-06 to 2007-11, serious violent hate crimes reported to police declined

The percentage of serious violent and property hate crimes reported to police declined from 2003-06 to 2007-11 (figure 5). However, the percentage of reported simple assault hate crimes did not change significantly across the two periods. The percentage of all types of nonhate crimes reported to police remained stable across both periods.

In 2007-11, the percentage of hate violent crimes reported to police was lower than the percentage of violent nonhate crimes reported. No differences were observed in the percentage of serious violent and simple assault hate and nonhate crimes reported to police in 2003-06. The percentage of property hate crimes reported to police was greater than the percentage of nonhate property crimes reported in 2003-06, but a similar percentage of hate and nonhate property crime was reported to police in 2007-11.

The percentage of violent hate crime victimizations that were unreported due to a belief that police could not or would not help increased from 2003-06 to 2007-11

The NCVS asks violent hate crime victims who did not report the crime to police why the crime was not reported. The reasons victims described as most important to them varied between 2003-06 and 2007-11. In 2003-06, the most common reason for not reporting the violent hate crime to police was that it was dealt with in another way (e.g., reported to an official other than law enforcement) or that the victim considered it a private or personal matter (35%). The percentage of victims who dealt with the crime another way or considered it a private matter declined in 2007-11 to 23% (figure 6).

In 2003-06, 14% of hate crime victims said they did not report the crime because they believed that the police could not or would not help, compared to 24% in 2007-11. A slightly higher percentage of violent hate crime victims stated that fear of reprisal or getting the offender in trouble was the most important reason for not reporting the crime to the police in 2007-11 (15%) than in 2003-06 (9%).

FIGURE 5

Hate and nonhate victimizations reported to the police, by type of crime, 2003–2006 and 2007–2011

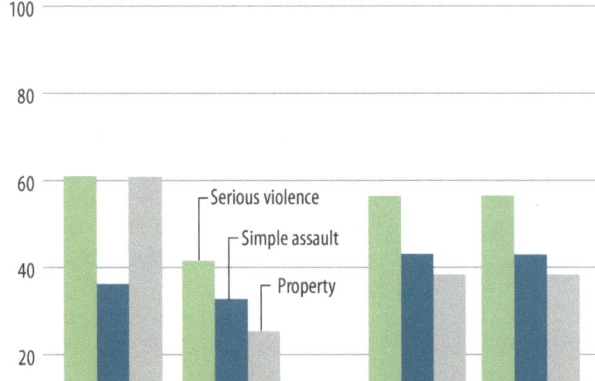

Note: Hate crime includes incidents confirmed by police as bias-motivated and incidents perceived by victims to be bias-motivated because the offender used hate language or left behind hate symbols. See appendix table 13 for estimates and standard errors.

Source: Bureau of Justice Statistics, National Crime Victimization Survey, 2003–2011.

FIGURE 6

Most important reason why violent hate crime victimization was not reported to police, 2003–2006 and 2007–2011

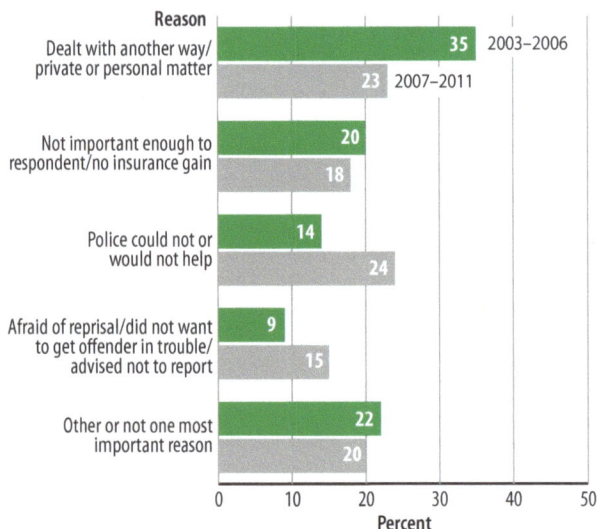

Note: Hate crime includes incidents confirmed by police as bias-motivated and incidents perceived by victims to be bias-motivated because the offender used hate language or left behind hate symbols. Based on violent hate crime victimizations not reported to police. See appendix table 14 for standard errors.

Source: Bureau of Justice Statistics, National Crime Victimization Survey, 2003–2011.

Whites, blacks, and Hispanics had similar rates of violent hate crime victimization in 2007-11

In 2003-06, Hispanics (1.4 per 1,000) experienced a higher rate of violent hate crime victimization than white non-Hispanics (0.8 per 1,000) and black non-Hispanics (0.5 per 1,000) (table 8). In 2007-11, the rate of violent hate crime victimization was similar for all three groups.

During both time periods, males consistently had a higher rate of violent hate crime victimization than females, and persons under age 18 experienced higher rates of victimization than adults age 18 or older. Persons in households with an income of under $25,000 per year consistently experienced a higher rate of violent hate crime victimization than persons in higher income categories in both time periods.

TABLE 8
Characteristics of violent hate crime victims, 2003–2006 and 2007–2011

Victim characteristic	Percent		Rate[a]	
	2003–2006	2007–2011	2003–2006	2007–2011
Sex	100%	100%		
Male	63	61	1.1	1.2
Female	37	39	0.6	0.7
Race/ethnicity	100%	100%		
White[b]	61	65	0.8	0.9
Black/African American[b]	7	13	0.5	1.0
Hispanic	20	15	1.4	1.0
American Indian/Alaska Native[b]	1 !	1 !	2.6 !	1.0 !
Asian/Native Hawaiian/other Pacific Islander[b]	3 !	3 !	0.5 !	0.7 !
Two or more races[b]	8 !	3 !	8.9 !	2.9 !
Age	100%	100%		
12–17	31	23	2.6	2.2
18–24	18	18	1.3	1.4
25–34	17	20	0.9	1.1
35–49	23	22	0.8	0.8
50–64	10	16	0.4	0.7
65 or older	1 !	2 !	0.1 !	0.1 !
Household income	100%	100%		
Less than $25,000	33	31	1.5	2.0
$25,000–$49,999	21	17	0.9	0.8
$50,000 or more	30	25	0.7	0.7
Not reported	16	27	0.6	0.9

Note: Hate crime includes incidents confirmed by police as bias-motivated and incidents perceived by victims to be bias-motivated because the offender used hate language or left behind hate symbols. Violent hate crimes include rape or sexual assault, robbery, aggravated assault, and simple assault. See appendix table 15 for standard errors.
! Interpret with caution; estimate based on 10 or fewer sample cases, or the coefficient of variation is greater than 50%.
[a]Per 1,000 persons age 12 or older in each category.
[b]Excludes persons of Hispanic or Latino origin.
Source: Bureau of Justice Statistics, National Crime Victimization Survey, 2003–2011.

The percentage of violent hate crimes committed by one offender declined from 70% in 2003-06 to 53% in 2007-11

The percentage of violent hate crimes committed by two or three offenders increased from 11% during 2003-06 to 25% during 2007-11, while the percentage committed by a single offender declined across the two time periods (table 9). The percentage of violent hate crime committed by a group of four or more offenders remained relatively stable.

TABLE 9
Characteristics of violent hate crime offenders as reported by victims, 2003–2006 and 2007–2011

Offender characteristic	2003–2006	2007–2011
Number of offenders	100%	100%
1	70	53
2 or 3	11	25
4 or more	13	16
Unknown	6 !	6
Sex	100%	100%
Male	70	65
Female	20	19
Both male and female	4 !	11
Unknown	6	6 !
Race[a]	100%	100%
White	37	53
Black	32	27
Other[b]	17	5
Various races[c]	6 !	7
Unknown	8	9
Age	100%	100%
17 or younger	25	22
18–29	20	19
30 or older	27	29
More than one age group	15	22
Unknown	13	9
Relationship to victim	100%	100%
Stranger	45	46
Intimate/family/casual acquaintance	43	46
Unknown	12	8

Note: Hate crime includes incidents confirmed by police as bias-motivated and incidents perceived by victims to be bias-motivated because the offender used hate language or left behind hate symbols. Detail may not sum to total due to rounding. See appendix table 16 for standard errors.

! Interpret with caution; estimate based on 10 or fewer sample cases, or the coefficient of variation is greater than 50%.

[a]Prior to 2011, data on the perceived Hispanic origin of offenders were not collected.

[b]Includes American Indian/Alaska Natives, Asians, and Pacific Islanders.

[c]Includes multiple offenders of more than one racial group.

Source: Bureau of Justice Statistics, National Crime Victimization Survey, 2003–2011.

The percentage of violent hate crime victims who perceived the offender to be white increased from 37% in 2003-06 to 53% in 2007-11. The age of offenders and the relationship between the victim and offender remained relatively unchanged across the two time periods. In 2007-11, about 46% of violent hate crime victims reported that the offender was a stranger, compared to 45% in 2003-06.

Police records indicate that hate crime incidents declined after a period of relative stability

According to the FBI's UCR hate crime data collection, 1,944 law enforcement agencies reported 6,222 hate crime incidents involving 7,713 victims in 2011. The remaining 87% of agencies that participated in the Hate Crime Statistics Program reported no hate crimes in their jurisdictions (not shown in a table).

Similar to the NCVS, the UCR showed a decline in the number of hate crime victimizations known to the police in 2011, compared to 2003. The number of hate crime victimizations known to the police declined by 15%, from 9,100 hate crime victimizations in 2003 to 7,700 in 2011 (figure 7).

FIGURE 7
Hate crime victimizations recorded in official police records, 2003–2011

Number of victimizations

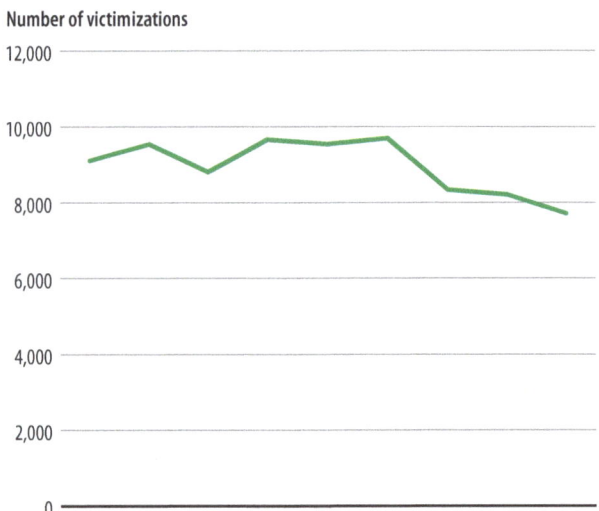

Note: Includes the following offenses: murder/non-negligent manslaughter, forcible rape, aggravated assault, simple assault, intimidation, other crimes against persons, robbery, burglary, larceny-theft, motor vehicle theft, arson, destruction/vandalism, other crimes against property, and crimes against society.

Source: Bureau of Justice Statistics, based on files provided by the FBI, Uniform Crime Reporting Program, Hate Crime Statistics, 2003–2011.

From 2003 to 2011, an average of seven hate crime homicides occurred each year

According to the UCR Hate Crime Reporting Program, four people were victims of hate crime homicides (murder or non-negligent manslaughter) in 2011 (not shown in table). Since a high of 14 homicides in 2003, the number of hate crime homicides ranged from three to nine victims each year between 2004 and 2011. This was an average of six homicides per year.

Property crimes accounted for 39% of hate crimes recorded in the UCR and 14% of hate crimes reported to police in the NCVS

From 2003 to 2011, rape, robbery, aggravated assault, and simple assault accounted for 32% of hate crimes reported to the UCR, compared to about 86% of hate crimes reported to police in the NCVS (table 10). Intimidation, a crime classification not recognized in the NCVS, accounted for 28% of the UCR hate crimes. About 39% of hate crime victimizations collected by the UCR were property crimes, such as burglary, theft, and vandalism. Vandalism, another crime not captured through the NCVS, accounted for about 86% of the UCR's property hate crimes (not shown in table).

TABLE 10
Hate crime victimizations recorded by the NCVS and UCR, by offense, 2003–2011

Hate crime offense	National Crime Victimization Survey			Uniform Crime Reporting Program
	Total	Not reported to police[a]	Reported to police[a]	
Violent crime	88.4%	90.3%	85.9%	60.2%
Homicide	~	~	~	0.1
Forcible rape[b]	2.1	2.8	1.1	0.1
Robbery	6.5	7.9	4.5!	1.9
Aggravated assault	18.0	12.1	27.2	10.6
Simple assault	61.7	67.4	53.1	19.0
Intimidation	~	~	~	27.8
Other[c]	~	~	~	0.2
Property crime	11.6%	9.7%	14.1%	39.4%
Burglary	4.8 !	1.1 !	10.2	1.9
Larceny-theft[d]	6.7	8.6	3.7 !	2.4
Motor vehicle theft	0.1	--	0.2	0.2
Vandalism	~	~	~	33.8
Other[e]	~	~	~	1.9
Other[f]	~%	~%	~%	0.4%

Note: See appendix table 17 for standard errors.

~Not applicable.

! Interpret data with caution. Estimates based on 10 or fewer sample cases, or the coefficient of variation is greater than 50%.

--Less than 0.05%.

[a]Excludes victims who did not know whether the hate crime was reported to the police.

[b]The NCVS also measures attempted and threatened rape and completed, attempted, and threatened sexual assault.

[c]Includes other violent offenses that are collected as part of the National Incident-Based Reporting System.

[d]Larceny is classified as a personal crime rather than property crime in the NCVS.

[e]Includes arson and property offenses not shown that are collected as part of the National Incident-Based Reporting System.

[f]Includes other offenses not shown that are collected as part of National Incident-Based Reporting System.

Source: Bureau of Justice Statistics, based on files provided by the FBI, Uniform Crime Reporting Program, Hate Crime Statistics, 2003–2011; Bureau of Justice Statistics, National Crime Victimization Survey, 2003–2011.

Offenders targeted victims because of racial bias against the victim in more than half of hate crime victimizations reported to the UCR

Similar to NCVS data, UCR data indicated that more than 50% of hate crime victims known to the police were targeted because of an offender's racial bias (figure 8). In both data collections, the percentage of hate crimes motivated by racial bias declined from 2003-06 to 2007-11. In 2007-11, UCR and NCVS data showed a similar percentage of hate crime victims targeted due to bias against religion and sexual orientation bias.

The percentage of hate crimes motivated by the victim's disability and the victim's ethnicity differed between the UCR and the NCVS. In 2007-11, the UCR identified about 1% of hate crime victimizations as motivated by bias against a victim's disability, compared to 14% identified in the NCVS. Similarly, bias against the victim's ethnicity was the motivation for 13% of hate crimes in the UCR, compared to 30% of hate crimes in the NCVS. One potential reason for the differences between the two sources is that while 60% of victims surveyed by the NCVS reported multiple perceived types of bias against them (not shown in a table), in the UCR about 0.1% of hate crime victims were recorded as being targeted for multiple sources of bias.

FIGURE 8

Offender bias in hate crimes recorded in official police records, 2003–2006 and 2007–2011

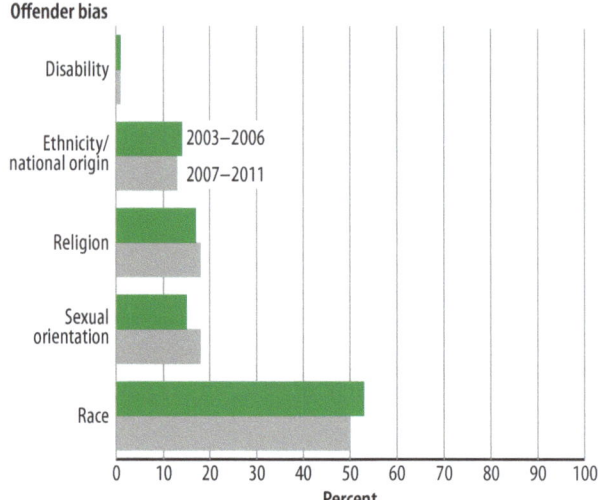

Note: In the Uniform Crime Reporting Program (UCR), a victim can include a person, business, institution, or society as a whole.

Source: Bureau of Justice Statistics, based on files provided by the FBI, Uniform Crime Report, Hate Crime Statistics, 2003–2011.

Methodology

National Crime Victimization Survey

The National Crime Victimization Survey (NCVS) is an annual data collection conducted by the U.S. Census Bureau for the Bureau of Justice Statistics (BJS). The NCVS collects information on nonfatal crimes, whether or not reported to the police, against persons age 12 or older in a nationally representative sample of household in the United States.

Survey results are based on data gathered from residents living throughout the United States, including persons living in group quarters, such as dormitories, rooming houses, and religious group dwellings. The survey excludes personnel living in military barracks and persons living in institutional settings, such as correctional or hospital facilities. For more detail, see the *Survey Methodology* for *Criminal Victimization in the United States, 2008,* NCJ 231173, BJS website, May 2011. Victim self-reports capture information about the number and characteristics of victimizations reported and not reported to law enforcement each year. Hate crime victimizations are based on victims' perceptions of the offenders' motivations. Victims provide evidence of the hate motivation by words, symbols, and actions used by the offenders.

Weighting adjustments for estimating household victimization

In 2011, about 79,800 households and 143,120 individuals age 12 or older were interviewed for the NCVS. The response rate was 90% for households and 88% of eligible individuals. Victimizations that occurred outside of the United States were excluded from this report.

Estimates in this report use data from the 1994 to 2011 NCVS data files. These files can be weighted to produce annual estimates of victimization for persons age 12 or older living in U.S. households. Because the NCVS relies on a sample rather than a census of the entire U.S. population, weights are designed to inflate sample point estimates to known population totals and to compensate for survey nonresponse and other aspects of the sample design.

The NCVS data files include both person and household weights. Person weights provide an estimate of the population represented by each person in the sample. Household weights provide an estimate of the total U.S. household population. Both household and person weights, after proper adjustment, are also typically used to form the denominator in calculations of crime rates.

Victimization weights used in this analysis account for the number of persons present during an incident and for repeat victims of series incidents. The weight counts series incidents as the actual number of incidents reported by the victim,

up to a maximum of 10 incidents. Series victimizations are similar in type but occur with such frequency that a victim is unable to recall each individual event or describe each event in detail. Survey procedures allow NCVS interviewers to identify and classify these similar victimizations as series victimizations and to collect detailed information on only the most recent incident in the series. In 2010, about 3% of all victimizations were series incidents. Weighting series incidents as the number of incidents up to a maximum of 10 incidents produces more reliable estimates of crime levels, while the cap at 10 minimizes the effect of extreme outliers on the rates. Additional information on the series enumeration is detailed in the report *Methods for Counting High Frequency Repeat Victimizations in the National Crime Victimization Survey*, NCJ 237308, BJS website, April 2012.

Year-to-year trend estimates are based on 2-year rolling averages centered on the most recent year. For example, estimates reported for 2011 represent the average estimates for 2010 and 2011. For other tables in this report, aggregate data for the time from 2003 through 2006, and 2007 through 2011 are the focus. These methods of analysis improve the reliability and stability of comparisons over time.

Standard error computations

Anytime national estimates are derived from a sample rather than the entire population, as is the case with the NCVS, caution is warranted when drawing conclusions about the size of one population estimate in comparison to another or about whether a time series of population estimates is changing. Estimates based on responses from a sample of the population each have some degree of sampling error. The sampling error, or margin of error, of an estimate depends on several factors, including the amount of variation in the responses, the size and representativeness of the sample, and the size of the subgroup for which the estimate is computed. One measure of the sampling error associated with an estimate is the standard error. The standard error can vary from one estimate to the next. In general, a smaller standard error provides a more reliable approximation of the true value than an estimate with a higher standard error. Estimates with relatively large standard errors are associated with less precision and reliability and should be interpreted with caution.

The coefficient of variation (CV) is a measure of an estimate's reliability. The CV is the ratio of the standard error to the estimate. In this report, the CV was calculated for all estimates. In cases where the CV was greater than 50% or the estimate was based on 10 or fewer sample cases, the estimate was noted with a "!" symbol (interpret data with caution; estimate based on 10 or fewer sample cases, or coefficient of variation is greater than 50%). A statistical test is used to determine whether differences in means or percentages are statistically significant once sampling error is taken into account. Comparisons made in the text were tested for statistical significance at the $p < .05$ level to ensure that the differences were larger than might be expected due to sampling variation.

Significance testing calculations were conducted at BJS using statistical programs developed specifically for the NCVS by the U.S. Census Bureau. These programs take into consideration many aspects of the complex NCVS sample design when calculating estimates. Standard errors for average annual estimates were calculated based on the ratio of the sums of victimizations and respondents across years. Many of the variables examined in this report may be related to one another and to other variables not included in the analyses. Complex relationships among variables were not fully explored in this report and warrant more extensive analysis. Readers are cautioned not to draw causal inferences based on the results presented.

Methodological changes to the NCVS in 2006

Methodological changes implemented in 2006 impacted the total violent crime estimates for that year to an extent that they were considered to be not comparable to estimates from other years. Evaluation of 2007 and later data from the NCVS conducted by BJS and the Census Bureau have found a high degree of confidence that estimates for 2007, 2008, and 2009 are consistent with and comparable to those for 2005 and previous years. The reports, *Criminal Victimization, 2006*, NCJ 219413, December 2007; *Criminal Victimization, 2007*, NCJ 224390, December 2008; *Criminal Victimization, 2008*, NCJ 227777, September 2009; *Criminal Victimization, 2009*, NCJ 231327, October 2010; *Criminal Victimization, 2010*, NCJ 235508, September 2011; and *Criminal Victimization, 2011*, NCJ 239437, October 2012, are available on the BJS website.

Although caution is warranted when comparing data from 2006 to other years, the aggregation of multiple years of data in this report diminishes the potential variation between 2006 and other years. In general, findings do not change significantly if data for 2006 are excluded.

Uniform Crime Reports (UCR)

The UCR Hate Crime Statistics Program captures information about the types of bias that motivate hate crimes, the nature of the offenses, and some information about the victims and offenders by attaching the collection of hate crime statistics to the established UCR data collection procedures. The hate crime data presented here comprise a subset of information that law enforcement agencies submit to the UCR Program.

Crimes reported to the FBI involve those motivated by biases based on race, religion, sexual orientation, ethnicity/ national origin, and disability. The 2012 UCR data collection will allow the reporting of crimes motivated by gender and gender identity bias, as well as crimes committed by and directed against juveniles. The victim of a hate crime may be an individual, business, institution, or society as a whole. In UCR data, law enforcement specifies the number of offenders and, when possible, the race of the offender or offenders as a group. Agencies that participated in the Hate Crime Statistics Program in 2011 represented nearly 285 million residents, or 92.3% percent of the nation's population. Their jurisdictions covered 49 states and the District of Columbia.

Hate crime legislation

On April 23, 1990, Congress passed the Hate Crime Statistics Act, which requires the Attorney General to collect data "about crimes that manifest evidence of prejudice based on race, religion, sexual orientation, or ethnicity." The Attorney General delegated the responsibilities of developing the procedures for implementing, collecting, and managing hate crime data to the director of the FBI, who in turn assigned the tasks to the UCR Program. Under the direction of the Attorney General and with the cooperation and assistance of many local and state law enforcement agencies, the UCR Program created a hate crime data collection to comply with the congressional mandate.

In September 1994, lawmakers amended the Hate Crime Statistics Act to include bias against persons with disabilities in the Violent Crime Control and Law Enforcement Act of 1994. The FBI started gathering data for the additional bias type on January 1, 1997.

The Church Arson Prevention Act, which was signed into law in July 1996, removed the sunset clause from the original statute and mandated that the collection of hate crime data become a permanent part of the UCR Program.

In 2009, Congress further amended the Hate Crime Statistics Act by passing the Matthew Shepard and James Byrd, Jr. Hate Crime Prevention Act. The amendment includes the collection of data for crimes motivated by bias against a particular gender and gender identity, as well as for crimes committed by, and crimes directed against, juveniles. The FBI is currently making plans to implement changes to collect these data.

The Hate Crime Statistics Act can be accessed at http://www. ssa.gov/OP_Home/comp2/D-USC-28.html.

APPENDIX TABLE 1
Population and total criminal victimization counts, 2003–2011

Year	U.S. resident population		Total criminal victimizations		
	Persons age 12 or older	Households	All[a]	Violent[b]	Property[c]
Total 2003–2011	2,242,945,200	1,073,766,700	224,845,600	59,401,600	162,270,300
2004	240,504,800	114,956,200	27,012,700	7,202,600	19,593,600
2005	243,104,500	116,437,700	26,097,800	6,836,900	19,034,100
2006	245,869,200	117,479,100	27,184,200	7,689,100	19,293,800
Total 2003–2006	972,748,100	464,870,700	108,393,800	29,783,300	77,774,800
2007	248,789,000	118,681,000	27,037,100	7,622,300	19,215,300
2008	251,293,700	120,322,300	24,699,300	6,603,800	17,897,000
2009	253,174,100	121,734,400	22,933,900	6,031,400	16,750,300
2010	255,033,800	122,606,400	21,255,700	5,302,600	15,817,300
2011	256,752,100	122,961,900	22,513,900	5,370,700	16,239,200
Total 2007–2011	1,270,197,200	608,896,000	116,451,800	29,618,300	84,495,500

Note: Estimates based on 2-year rolling averages centered on the most recent year. Numbers rounded to the nearest hundred.

[a]Includes violent crimes, personal larceny, and household property crimes.

[b]Includes rape or sexual assault, robbery, aggravated assault, and simple assault.

[c]Includes burglary, motor vehicle theft, and other theft.

Source: Bureau of Justice Statistics, National Crime Victimization Survey, 2003–2011.

APPENDIX TABLE 2
Estimates and standard errors for figure 1: Victim perceptions of offender motivation in hate crime, 2003–2006 and 2007–2011

Offender motivation	Percent		Standard errors	
	2003–2006	2007–2011	2003–2006	2007–2011
Perceived characteristics	14%	13%	2.5%	1.8%
Disability	10	14	2.2	1.8
Gender	15	18	2.6	2.1
Sexual orientation	16	18	2.7	2.1
Religion	10	21	2.1	2.2
Ethnicity	27	30	3.2	2.5
Association	29	31	3.3	2.5
Race	63	54	3.6	2.7

Source: Bureau of Justice Statistics, National Crime Victimization Survey, 2003–2011.

APPENDIX TABLE 4
Standard errors for table 1: Violent hate crimes with crimes motivated by gender bias excluded and included, 2010–2011

Year	Number		Rate per 1,000 persons age 12 or older	
	Excluding gender bias	Including gender bias	Excluding gender bias	Including gender bias
2010	30,247	30,507	0.1	0.1
2011	30,689	31,945	0.1	0.1

Source: Bureau of Justice Statistics, National Crime Victimization Survey, 2010–2011.

APPENDIX TABLE 3
Estimates and stardard errors for figure 2: Rate of violent hate crime victimizations, by method used to count high frequency repeat (series) victimizations, 2004–2011

Year	Rate per 1,000 persons age 12 or older		Standard error	
	Series = 1	Series = number of incidents up to 10	Series = 1	Series = number of incidents up to 10
2004	0.7	0.9	0.1	0.1
2005	0.6	0.8	0.1	0.1
2006	0.8	0.9	0.1	0.1
2007	0.8	1.0	0.1	0.1
2008	0.7	1.0	0.1	0.1
2009	0.6	1.1	0.1	0.1
2010	0.5	1.0	0.1	0.1
2011	0.6	0.8	0.1	0.1

Source: Bureau of Justice Statistics, National Crime Victimization Survey, 2003–2011.

APPENDIX TABLE 5
Standard errors for table 2: Hate crime victimizations, 2004–2011

Year	Total hate crimes		Violent hate crimes			Property hate crimes		
	Annual average	Percent of total victimizations	Annual average	Rate	Percent of total violent victimizations	Annual average	Rate	Percent of total property victimizations
2004	38,150	0.1%	33,292	0.1	0.3%	16,218	0.1	0.1%
2005	36,153	0.1	33,915	0.1	0.4	9,298	0.1	0.0
2006	36,840	0.1	35,175	0.1	0.3	7,375	0.0	0.0
2007	39,039	0.1	36,798	0.1	0.3	10,435	0.1	0.0
2008	38,338	0.1	36,306	0.1	0.4	9,819	0.1	0.0
2009	42,075	0.1	40,625	0.1	0.5	8,512	0.1	0.0
2010	41,847	0.1	40,334	0.1	0.5	8,072	0.0	0.0
2011	31,065	0.1	29,258	0.1	0.4	9,757	0.1	0.0

Source: Bureau of Justice Statistics, National Crime Victimization Survey, 2003–2011.

APPENDIX TABLE 6
Standard errors for table 3: Annual average for hate crime victimizations, 2003–2006 and 2007–2011

	Annual average hate crimes	
Annual average	2003–2006	2007–2011
Number	38,431	31,988
Violent	35,066	30,504
Property	11,207	10,771
Percent		
Total crime	0.1%	0.1%
Violent crime	0.2	0.2
Property crime	0.0	0.0
Rate		
Violent	0.1	0.1
Property	0.0	0.0

Source: Bureau of Justice Statistics, National Crime Victimization Survey, 2003–2011.

APPENDIX TABLE 7
Standard errors for table 4: Hate crime victimizations, by type of crime, 2003–2006 and 2007–2011

Type of crime	2003–2006	2007–2011
Violent	2.7%	1.5%
Serious violent	3.1	2.5
Rape and sexual assault	0.6 !	0.6 !
Robbery	1.2 !	1.3
Aggravated assault	2.5	2.1
Simple assault	3.5	2.8
Property	2.0%	1.8%
Burglary	1.5	0.9 !
Theft	1.4	1.6

! Interpret with caution; estimate based on 10 or fewer sample cases, or the coefficient of variation is greater than 50%.

Source: Bureau of Justice Statistics, National Crime Victimization Survey, 2003–2011.

APPENDIX TABLE 8
Estimates and standard errors for figure 3: Hate and nonhate victimizations, by type of crime, 2003–2011

Type of crime	Percent		Standard error	
	Hate	Nonhate	Hate	Nonhate
Serious violent	27%	9%	1.8%	0.2%
Simple assault	62	17	2.1	0.2
Property	11	73	1.6	0.4

Source: Bureau of Justice Statistics, National Crime Victimization Survey, 2003–2011.

APPENDIX TABLE 9
Standard errors for table 5: Presence of weapons and injuries sustained in violent hate crime victimizations, 2003–2006 and 2007–2011

	2003–2006	2007–2011
Weapon		
Yes	3.2%	2.4%
No	3.8	2.7
Don't know	2.4	1.5
Injury		
None	3.5%	2.2%
Any	3.4	2.1

Source: Bureau of Justice Statistics, National Crime Victimization Survey, 2003–2011.

APPENDIX TABLE 10
Standard errors for table 6: Hate crime victimizations, by location, 2003–2006 and 2007–2011

Location	2003–2006	2007–2011
At or near victim's home	3.4%	2.5%
At or near friend or relative's home	1.6	0.8
Commercial place	2.3	2.0
Parking lot/street/public transportation	2.9	2.3
School	3.1	2.1
Other	2.1	1.2

Source: Bureau of Justice Statistics, National Crime Victimization Survey, 2003–2011.

APPENDIX TABLE 11
Estimates and standard errors for figure 4: Violent hate and nonhate victimizations, by location, 2003–2011

	Percent		Standard error	
Location	Hate	Nonhate	Hate	Nonhate
At or near victim's home	27%	36%	1.9%	0.5%
At or near friend or relative's home	4	8	0.8	0.2
Commercial place	16	11	1.5	0.3
Parking lot/on street/ public transportation	24	22	1.8	0.4
School	22	13	1.7	0.3
Other	7	10	1.1	0.3

Source: Bureau of Justice Statistics, National Crime Victimization Survey, 2003–2011.

APPENDIX TABLE 12
Standard errors for table 7: Hate crime victimizations reported to police, 2003–2006 and 2007–2011

	Total		Violent	
	2003–2006	2007–2011	2003–2006	2007–2011
Reported by—	3.7%	2.6%	4.0%	2.7%
Victim	3.2	2.3	3.1	2.4
Someone else	3.0	1.6	3.4	1.7
Complaint signed	2.3%	1.6%	2.6%	1.7%
Arrest made	2.0%	1.1%	2.3%	1.1%
Not reported	3.7%	2.6%	4.0%	2.8%

Source: Bureau of Justice Statistics, National Crime Victimization Survey, 2003–2011.

APPENDIX TABLE 13
Estimates and standard errors for figure 5: Hate and nonhate victmizations reported to police, by type of crime, 2003–2006 and 2007–2011

	Percent				Standard errors			
	Hate		Nonhate		Hate		Nonhate	
Type of crime	2003–2006	2007–2011	2003–2006	2007–2011	2003–2006	2007–2011	2003–2006	2007–2011
Serious violence	61%	42%	57%	57%	7.3%	4.8%	1.3%	1.2%
Simple assault	36	33	43	43	4.3	3.3	1.0	0.9
Property	61	25	38	38	7.0	9.9	0.5	0.6

Source: Bureau of Justice Statistics, National Crime Victimization Survey, 2003–2011.

APPENDIX TABLE 14
Standard errors for figure 6: Most important reason why violent hate crime victimization was not reported to police, 2003–2006 and 2007–2011

	Percent		Standard error	
Reason	2003–2006	2007–2011	2003–2006	2007–2011
Dealt with another way/private or personal matter	35%	23%	5.0%	2.9%
Not important enough to respondent/no insurance gain	20	18	4.2	2.7
Police could not or would not help	14	24	3.6	3.0
Afraid of reprisal/did not want to get offender in trouble/advised not to report	9	15	2.9	2.5
Other or not one most important reason	22	20	4.4	2.7

Source: Bureau of Justice Statistics, National Crime Victimization Survey, 2003–2011.

Standard errors for table 8: Characteristics of violent hate crime victims, 2003–2006 and 2007–2011

Victim characteristic	Percent		Rate	
	2003–2006	2007–2011	2003–2006	2007–2011
Sex				
Male	3.9%	2.8%	0.12	0.09
Female	3.9	2.8	0.09	0.07
Race/ethnicity				
White	3.9%	2.7%	0.08	0.07
Black/African American	1.9	1.9	0.15	0.16
Hispanic	3.2	2.0	0.25	0.15
American Indian/Alaska Native	0.9	0.4	1.76	0.73
Asian/Native Hawaiian/other Pacific Islander	1.2	1.0	0.26	0.20
Two or more races	2.1	0.9	2.46	0.88
Age				
12–17	3.7%	2.4%	0.39	0.27
18–24	3.0	2.1	0.26	0.19
25–34	3.0	2.2	0.18	0.15
35–49	3.3	2.3	0.13	0.10
50–64	2.4	2.0	0.11	0.10
65 or older	0.7	0.7	0.05	0.05
Household income				
Less than $25,000	3.7%	2.6%	0.22	0.21
$25,000–$49,999	3.2	2.1	0.15	0.11
$50,000 or more	3.6	2.4	0.11	0.08
Not reported	2.9	2.5	0.13	0.10

Source: Bureau of Justice Statistics, National Crime Victimization Survey, 2003–2011.

Standard errors for table 9: Characteristics of violent hate crime offenders as reported by victims, 2003–2006 and 2007–2011

Offender characteristic	2003–2006	2007–2011
Number of offenders		
1	3.7%	2.9%
2 or 3	2.5	2.4
4 or more	2.6	2.0
Unknown	1.8	1.3
Sex		
Male	3.7%	2.7%
Female	3.2	2.2
Both male and female	1.5	1.7
Unknown	1.9	1.3
Race		
White	3.9%	2.9%
Black	3.7	2.5
Other	2.9	1.2
Various races	1.8	1.4
Unknown	2.1	1.5
Age		
17 or younger	3.4%	2.3%
18–29	3.1	2.2
30 or older	3.5	2.6
More than one age group	2.8	2.3
Unknown	2.7	1.5
Relationship to victim		
Stranger	4.0%	2.8%
Intimate/family/casual acquaintance	4.0	2.8
Unknown	2.5	1.5

Source: Bureau of Justice Statistics, National Crime Victimization Survey, 2003–2011.

Standard errors for table 10: Hate crime victimizations recorded by the NCVS and UCR, by offense, 2003–2011

Hate crime offense	National Crime Victimization Survey		
	Total	Not reported to police	Reported to police
Violent crime	1.3%	1.6%	2.2%
Homicide	~	~	~
Forcible rape	0.4	0.6	0.4
Robbery	0.9	1.3	1.2 !
Aggravated assault	1.5	1.6	2.7
Simple assault	2.1	2.6	3.3
Intimidation	~	~	~
Other violent	~	~	~
Property crime	1.6%	2.0%	2.8%
Burglary	0.8 !	0.5 !	1.7
Larceny-theft	1.3	1.9	1.6 !
Motor vehicle theft	0.1	~	0.3
Vandalism	~	~	~
Other property	~	~	~
Other	~	~	~

~Not applicable.

! Interpret with caution; estimate based on 10 or fewer sample cases, or the coefficient of variation is greater than 50%.

Source: Bureau of Justice Statistics, National Crime Victimization Survey, 2003–2011.

The Bureau of Justice Statistics is the statistics agency of the U.S. Department of Justice. William J. Sabol is acting director.

This report was written by Nathan Sandholtz, Lynn Langton, and Michael Planty. Erika Harrell verified the report.

Catherine Bird and Jill Thomas edited the report, and Barbara Quinn produced the report under the supervision of Doris J. James.

March 2013, NCJ 241291

NCJ 241291

Office of Justice Programs
Innovation • Partnerships • Safer Neighborhoods
www.ojp.usdoj.gov

www.ingramcontent.com/pod-product-compliance
Lightning Source LLC
Chambersburg PA
CBHW050913180526
45159CB00007B/2901